Content

Color Fusion Blanket

Row upon row of pretty stitches in alternating little-girl shades create a lovely blanket that will be cherished for years to come.

Designed by Kimberley Biddix

Finished Measurements

Blanket measures approximately 35" x 47" long (89cm x 119.5cm)

Gauge

In pattern, 3 pattern repeats and 6½ rows = 4"/10cm. **Note:** One pattern repeat consists of [dc, Cl, dc, ch 1] or one 3-dc group and the following ch-1. Gauge is not critical for this project.

Stitches Used

Chain (**ch**)
Double crochet (**dc**)
Half double crochet (**hdc**)
Single crochet (**sc**)
Slip stitch (**sl st**)

Special Terms

Ldc Long double crochet—Yarn over; working over next ch-1 sp, insert hook in indicated ch-1 sp 2 rows below, yarn over and draw up a loop (to current row height), [yarn over and draw through 2 loops on hook] twice.

Cl Cluster—Yarn over, insert hook in indicated stitch and draw up a loop, yarn over and draw through 2 loops on hook (2 loops remain on hook), [yarn over, insert hook in same stitch and draw up a loop, yarn over and draw through 2 loops on hook] 3 times, yarn over and draw through all 5 loops on hook.

Note:
To change color, work last stitch of old color to last yarn over, yarn over with new color and draw through all loops on hook to complete stitch. Proceed with new color. Fasten off old color.

Blanket

With A, ch 98.

What you'll need:

YARN
Caron International's Simply Soft Collection (100% acrylic)
6 oz (A), 6 oz (B), 12 oz (C), 6 oz (D), 6 oz (E)
Shown in: #9737 Light Country Peach (A), #9717 Orchid (B), #9701 White (C), #9719 Soft Pink (D), #0712 Soft Blue (E)

CROCHET HOOK
One size US H-8 (5mm), or size to obtain gauge

ADDITIONAL MATERIALS
Yarn needle

Row 1 (RS) Dc in 6th ch from hook (beginning ch counts as dc, ch 1), dc in next 2 ch, *ch 1, sk next ch, dc in next 3 ch; repeat from * across to last 2 ch, ch 1, sk next ch, dc in last ch, turn—Twenty-three 3-dc groups.

Row 2 Ch 4 (counts as dc, ch 1 here and throughout), sk first ch-1 sp, dc in next dc, Cl in next dc, dc in next dc, *ch 1, sk next ch-1 sp, dc in next dc, Cl in next dc, dc in next dc; repeat from * across to turning ch-sp , ch 1, dc in 4th ch of turning ch and change to B, turn—23 clusters. Fasten off A.

Row 3 Ch 3 (counts as first dc here and throughout), Ldc in next ch-1 sp of Row 1 (2 rows below), dc in next dc, ch 1, sk next Cl, dc in next dc, *Ldc in next ch-1 sp 2 rows below, dc in next dc, ch 1, sk next Cl, dc in next dc; repeat from * across to turning ch-sp, Ldc in next ch-1 sp 2 rows below, dc in 3rd ch of turning ch, turn.

Row 4 Ch 3, Cl in next dc, *dc in next dc, ch 1, sk next ch-1 sp, dc in next dc, Cl in next dc; repeat from * across to turning ch, dc in top of turning ch and change to C, turn. Fasten off B.

Row 5 Ch 4, sk first Cl, *dc in next dc, Ldc in next ch-1 sp 2 rows below, dc in next dc, ch 1, sk next Cl; repeat from * across to turning ch,

dc in top of turning ch, turn.

Row 6 Ch 4, sk first ch-1 sp, dc in next dc, Cl in next dc, dc in next dc, *ch 1, sk next ch-1 sp, dc in next dc, Cl in next dc, dc in next dc; repeat from * across to turning ch-sp , ch 1, dc in 3rd ch of turning ch and change to D, turn. Fasten off C.

Rows 7 and 8 With D, repeat Rows 3 and 4; change to E in last st of Row 8. Fasten off D.

Rows 9 and 10 With E, repeat Rows 5 and 6; change to C in last st of Row 10. Fasten off E.

Rows 11 and 12 With C, repeat Rows 3 and 4; change to A in last st of Row 12. Fasten off C.

Rows 13 and 14 With A, repeat Rows 5 and 6; change to B in last st of Row 14. Fasten off A.

Rows 15 and 16 With B, repeat Rows 3 and 4; change to C in last st of Row 16. Fasten off B.

Rows 17 and 18 With C, repeat Rows 5 and 6; change to D in last st of Row 18. Fasten off C.

Rows 19–66 Repeat Rows 7–18 four more times.

Rows 67–72 Repeat Rows 7–12.
Do not change color at end of Row 72.
Do not fasten off.

Edging

Rnd 1 (RS) Continuing with C, ch 1, sc evenly spaced around all edges of blanket, working 3 sc in each corner; join with sl st in first sc and change to A, do not turn. Fasten off C.

Rnd 2 Ch 2, hdc in each sc around, working 3 hdc in each corner; join with sl st in top of beginning ch and change to B. Fasten off A.

Rnd 3 With B, repeat Round 2. Fasten off B.

Finishing

Using yarn needle, weave in all ends. Block gently, if desired. ■

Just Ducky Blanket

Lemon-yellow ducks that evoke baby's favorite bath toy swim across an ocean-blue sea of single and double crochet.

Designed by Kimberley Biddix

What you'll need:

YARN
Caron International's Simply Soft Collection
(100% acrylic) 12 oz (A), 12 oz (B)
Shown in: #0004 Blueberry (A), #0017 Lemon (B)

CROCHET HOOK
One size US H-8 (5mm), or size to obtain gauge

ADDITIONAL MATERIALS
Yarn needle

Finished Measurements

Blanket measures approximately 40" x 36"/101.5cm x 91.5cm

Gauge

In double crochet, 16 sts and 7 rows = 4"/10cm.
Gauge is not critical for this project.

Stitches Used

Chain (**ch**)
Double crochet (**dc**)
Single crochet (**sc**)
Slip stitch (**sl st**)

Note:
To change color, work last stitch of old color to last yarn over. Yarn over with new color and draw through all loops on hook to complete stitch. Proceed with new color. Fasten off old color.

Helpful Hint:
Weave in ends as work progresses, to reduce the amount of finishing work.

Blanket

With A, ch 145.
Note Work in duck pattern following instructions below and/or the chart on next page.
Row 1 (RS) Dc in 4th ch (beginning ch counts as first dc) from hook and in each remaining ch across, turn—143 dc.
Row 2 Ch 3, dc in each dc across, turn.

Begin Filet Pattern

Rows 3 and 4 Ch 3, dc in next 3 dc, ch 1, sk next dc, dc in next 4 dc, *[ch 1, sk next dc, dc in next dc] 20 times, dc in next 3 dc; repeat from * 2 more times, ch 1, sk next dc, dc in next 4 dc, turn.
Note: In following rows, a dc and a ch-1 sp are each a "st."
Row 5 Ch 3, dc in next 3 dc, ch 1, sk next ch-1 sp, dc in next 4 dc, *[ch 1, sk next ch-1 sp, dc in next dc] 6 times, ch 1; change to B, sk next ch-1 sp, dc in next 13 sts; change to A, [ch 1, sk next ch-1 sp, dc in next dc] 7 times, dc in next 3 dc; repeat from * 2 more times, ch 1, sk next ch-1 sp, dc in next 4 dc, turn.
Row 6 Ch 3, dc in next 3 dc, ch 1, sk next ch-1 sp, dc in next 4 dc, *[ch 1, sk next ch-1 sp, dc in next dc] 5 times, ch 1; change to B, sk next ch-1 sp, dc in next 17 sts; change to A, [ch 1, sk next ch-1 sp, dc in next dc] 6 times, dc in next 3 dc; repeat from * 2 more times, ch 1, sk next ch-1 sp, dc in next 4 dc, turn.
Row 7 Ch 3, dc in next 3 dc, ch 1, sk next ch-1 sp, dc in next 4 dc, *[ch 1, sk next ch-1 sp, dc in next dc] 4 times, ch 1; change to B, sk next ch-1 sp, dc in next 21 sts; change to A, [ch 1, sk next ch-1 sp, dc in next dc] 5 times, dc in next 3 dc; repeat from * 2 more times, ch 1, sk next ch-1 sp, dc in next 4 dc, turn.
Rows 8–12 Ch 3, dc in next 3 dc, ch 1, sk next ch-1 sp, dc in next 4 dc, *[ch 1, sk next ch-1 sp, dc in next dc] 3 times, ch 1; change to B, sk next ch-1 sp, dc in next 25 sts; change to A, [ch 1, sk next ch-1 sp, dc in next

dc] 4 times, dc in next 3 dc; repeat from * 2 more times, ch 1, sk next ch-1 sp, dc in next 4 dc, turn.
Row 13 Ch 3, dc in next 3 dc, ch 1, sk next ch-1 sp, dc in next 4 dc, *[ch 1, sk next ch-1 sp, dc in next dc] 4 times, ch 1; change to B, sk next ch-1 sp, dc in next 11 sts; change to A, [ch 1, sk next ch-1 sp, dc in next dc] 3 times, ch 1; change to B, sk next ch-1 sp, dc in next 5 sts; change to A, [ch 1, sk next ch-1 sp, dc in next dc] 4 times, dc in next 3 dc; repeat from * 2 more times, ch 1, sk next ch-1 sp, dc in next 4 dc, turn.
Row 14 Ch 3, dc in next 3 dc, ch 1, sk next ch-1 sp, dc in next 4 dc, *[ch 1, sk next ch-1 sp, dc in next dc] 11 times, ch 1; change to B, sk next ch-1 sp, dc in next 5 sts; change to A, [ch 1, sk next ch-1 sp, dc in next dc] 6 times, dc in next 3 dc; repeat from * 2 more times, ch 1, sk next ch-1 sp, dc in next 4 dc, turn.
Row 15 Ch 3, dc in next 3 dc, ch 1, sk next ch-1 sp, dc in next 4 dc, *ch 1, sk next ch-1 sp, dc in next dc, ch 1; change to B, sk next ch-1 sp, dc in next 15 sts; change to A, [ch 1, sk next ch-1 sp, dc in next dc] 11 times, dc in next 3 dc; repeat from * 2 more times, ch 1, sk next ch-1 sp, dc in next 4 dc, turn.
Row 16 Ch 3, dc in next 3 dc, ch 1, sk next ch-1 sp, dc in next 4 dc, *[ch 1, sk next ch-1 sp, dc in next dc] 9 times, ch 1; change to B, sk next ch-1 sp, dc in next 15 sts; change to A, [ch 1, sk next ch-1 sp, dc in next dc] 3 times, dc in next 3 dc; repeat from * 2 more times, ch 1, sk next ch-1 sp, dc in next 4 dc, turn.
Row 17 Ch 3, dc in next 3 dc, ch 1, sk next ch-1 sp, dc in next 4 dc, *[ch 1, sk next ch-1 sp, dc in next dc] 3 times, ch 1; change to B, sk next ch-1 sp, dc in next 13 sts; change to A,

[ch 1, sk next ch-1 sp, dc in next dc] 10 times, dc in next 3 dc; repeat from * 2 more times, ch 1, sk next ch-1 sp, dc in next 4 dc, turn.

Row 18 Ch 3, dc in next 3 dc, ch 1, sk next ch-1 sp, dc in next 4 dc, *[ch 1, sk next ch-1 sp, dc in next dc] 9 times, ch 1; change to B, sk next ch-1 sp, dc in next 13 sts; change to A, [ch 1, sk next ch-1 sp, dc in next dc] 4 times, dc in next 3 dc; repeat from * 2 more times, ch 1, sk next ch-1 sp, dc in next 4 dc, turn.

Row 19 Ch 3, dc in next 3 dc, ch 1, sk next ch-1 sp, dc in next 4 dc, *[ch 1, sk next ch-1 sp, dc in next dc] 4 times, ch 1; change to B, sk next ch-1 sp, dc in next 9 sts; change to A, [ch 1, sk next ch-1 sp, dc in next dc] 11 times, dc in next 3 dc; repeat from * 2 more times, ch 1, sk next ch-1 sp, dc in next 4 dc, turn.

Row 20 Ch 3, dc in next 3 dc, ch 1, sk next ch-1 sp, dc in next 4 dc, *[ch 1, sk next ch-1 sp, dc in next dc] 11 times, ch 1; change to B, sk next ch-1 sp, dc in next 5 sts; change to A, [ch 1, sk next ch-1 sp, dc in next dc] 6 times, dc in next 3 dc; repeat from * 2 more times, ch 1, sk next ch-1 sp, dc in next 4 dc, turn.

Rows 21 and 22 Repeat Row 3.

Rows 23 and 24 Ch 3, dc in next 3 dc, ch 1, sk next ch-1 sp, dc in each st across to last 5 sts, ch 1, sk next ch-1 sp, dc in last 4 sts, turn.

Repeat Rows 3–24 once more.

Repeat Rows 3–22 once more.

Next Row Ch 3, dc in each dc and ch-1 sp across, turn.

Last Row Ch 3, dc in each dc across. Fasten off.

Finishing

Border

With RS facing, join B with sl st in edge of blanket.

Rnd 1 Ch 1, sc evenly spaced all the way around outer edge, working 2 sc in each corner; join with sl st in first sc.

Rnd 2 Ch 1, sc in each sc around, working 2 sc in each corner. Fasten off.

Bow: Cut 4"/10cm length of A. Attach length to duck in middle of neck. Tie length in a bow and trim. Repeat for each duck.

Eye: With A, and referring to photograph for placement, embroider a French knot for eye. Repeat for each duck.

Using yarn needle, weave in ends. Block gently, if desired. ▪

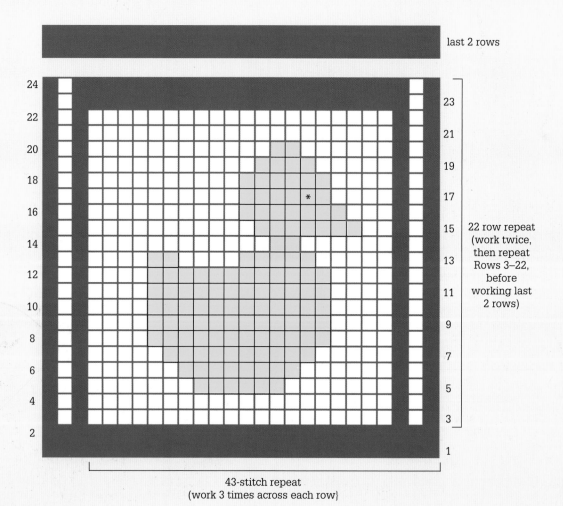

last 2 rows

22 row repeat (work twice, then repeat Rows 3–22, before working last 2 rows)

43-stitch repeat (work 3 times across each row)

■ solid block worked with A
☐ open block worked with A
☐ solid block worked with B
✱ French knot worked with A (for eye)

solid block = dc in next st (dc or ch-1 sp), dc in next dc
open block = ch 1, sk next st (dc or ch-1 sp), dc in next dc

Sunrise Blanket

Happy colors make for a happy baby. Arrange these simple squares as we did or as you please.

Designed by Ira Dearing

Finished Measurements

Blanket measures approximately 40½" x 40½"/103cm x 103cm

Gauge

One block measures approximately 6¼" x 6¼"/16 x 16cm. *Gauge is not critical for this project.*

Stitches Used

Chain (**ch**)
Half double crochet (**hdc**)
Single crochet (**sc**)
Slip stitch (**sl st**)

Special Stitch

long-sc: Long single crochet—Insert hook in indicated stitch 2 rows below, yarn over and draw up a loop (to current row height), yarn over and draw through 2 loops on hook. **Notes:** Do not work into the corresponding stitch in the current working row. A stitch "2 rows below" is in the row immediately below the row into which a stitch would usually be worked.

Notes

1. Blanket is made from 36 blocks, arranged in 6 rows of 6 squares each.
2. Each sc, ch-1, and long-sc count as one stitch each.

Block

(make 36 – 2 with A, 6 with F, and 7 each with B, C, D, and E)
Ch 26.
Row 1 (RS) Working in back bumps, sc in

What you'll need:

YARN

Caron International's Simply Soft (100% acrylic) 6 oz (A), 6 oz (B), 6 oz (C), 6 oz (D), 6 oz (E), 6 oz (F)
Shown in: #9701 White (A), #9719 Soft Pink (B), #9717 Orchid (C), #9712 Soft Blue (D), #9726 Soft Yellow (E), #9737 Light Country Peach (F)

CROCHET HOOK

One size US J-10 (6mm), or size to obtain gauge

ADDITIONAL MATERIALS

Yarn needle

2nd ch from hook and in each remaining ch across, turn—25 sc.
Row 2 Ch 1, sc in each sc across, turn.
Row 3 Ch 1, sc in first sc, *ch 1, sk next st, long-sc in next st 2 rows below; repeat from * across to last 2 sts, ch 1, sk next st, sc in last sc, turn.
Row 4 Ch 1, sc in first sc, *long-sc in next st 2 rows below, ch 1, sk next st; repeat from * across to last 2 sts, long-sc in next st 2 rows below, sc in last sc, turn.
Rows 5–28 Repeat last 2 rows 12 times.
Row 29 Ch 1, sc in first 2 sts, *long-sc in next st 2 rows below, sc in next st; repeat from * across to last st, sc in last st, turn.
Row 30 Ch 1, sc in each sc across. Fasten off.

Finishing

With RS facing and all blocks facing in the same direction, arrange blocks into 6 rows of 6 blocks each, as shown in assembly diagram. Whipstitch blocks together.

Border

Rnd 1 With RS facing, join A with sl st in edge of blanket, sc evenly spaced all the way around the outer edge, working 3 sc in each corner; join with sl st in first sc.
Rnds 2–4 Ch 2, hdc in each st around, working 3 hdc in center st of each corner; join with sl st in top of beginning ch. Fasten off. Using yarn needle, weave in ends. Block gently, if desired. ■

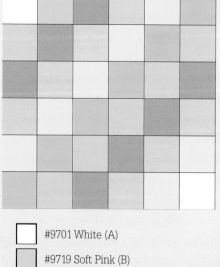

- ⬜ #9701 White (A)
- ⬜ #9719 Soft Pink (B)
- ⬜ #9717 Orchid (C)
- ⬜ #9712 Soft Blue (D)
- ⬜ #9726 Soft Yellow (E)
- ⬜ #9737 Light Country Peach (F)

Stairsteps Blanket

The bright color palette and bold design make this coverlet the perfect gift for a thoroughly modern mom.

Designed by Renée Barnes

What you'll need:

YARN
Caron International's Simply Soft Collection (100% acrylic)
6 oz (A), 6 oz (B), 6 oz (C), 6 oz (D), 6 oz (E), 6 oz (F)
Shown in: #0017 Lemon (A), #0016 Melon (B), #0015 Strawberry (C), #0003 Pistachio (D), #0005 Blackberry (E), #0004 Blueberry (F)

CROCHET HOOK
One size US H-8 (5mm), or size to obtain gauge

ADDITIONAL MATERIALS
Yarn needle

Finished Measurements
Blanket measures approximately 32" wide x 32" long (81.5cm x 81.5cm)

Gauge
In single crochet, 13 sts and 10 rows = 4"/10cm.
One square measures 5" x 5"/ 12.5 x 12.5cm.
Gauge is not critical for this project.

Stitches Used
Chain (**ch**)
Half double crochet (**hdc**)
Single crochet (**sc**)
Slip stitch (**sl st**)

Square
(make a total of 36 in indicated colors)
Color Sequence #1 (make 2): Work Rounds 1–3 with A, work Rows 4–10 with B.
Color Sequence #2 (make 6): Work Rounds 1–3 with D, work Rows 4–10 with C.
Color Sequence #3 (make 2): Work Rounds 1–3 with C, work Rows 4–10 with D.
Color Sequence #4 (make 4): Work Rounds 1–3 with E, work Rows 4–10 with D.
Color Sequence #5 (make 6): Work Rounds 1–3 with F, work Rows 4–10 with E.
Color Sequence #6 (make 2): Work Rounds 1–3 with E, work Rows 4–10 with F.
Color Sequence #7 (make 4): Work Rounds 1–3 with A, work Rows 4–10 with F.
Color Sequence #8 (make 6): Work Rounds 1–3 with B, work Rows 4–10 with A.
Color Sequence #9 (make 4): Work Rounds 1–3 with C, work Rows 4–10 with B.

Inner Square
With first color, ch 4; join with sl st in first ch to form a ring.

Rnd 1 (RS) Ch 1, [3 sc in ring, ch 2] 4 times; join with sl st in first sc—12 sc and 4 ch-2 sp.
Rnd 2 Ch 2 (counts as first hdc here and throughout), hdc in next 2 sc, (hdc, ch 3, hdc) in next ch-2 sp (corner made), *hdc in next 3 sc, (hdc, ch 3, hdc) in next ch-2 sp (corner made); repeat from * 2 more times; join with sl st in top of beginning ch—20 hdc and 4 ch-3 sp.
Rnd 3 Ch 2, hdc in next 3 hdc, (hdc, ch 3,

A		F		E		D		C		#1	A
B	#8	A	#7	F	#5	E	#4	D	#2		B
B		A		F		E		#3	C	C	
C	#9	B	#8	A	#7	F	#5		D	D	#2
C		B		A		#6	E	E			D
D	#2	C	#9	B	#8		F	F	#5	E	#4
D		C		#1	A	A		F		E	
E	#4	D	#2		B	B	#8	A	#7	F	#5
E		#3	C	C		B		A		F	
F	#5		D	D	#2	C	#9	B	#8	A	#7
F		E		D		C		B		A	
E	#6	F	#5	E	#4	D	#2	C	#9	B	#8

Note: In each square, the number indicates the color sequence, the letter in the small box indicates the color of the inner square, and other letter indicates the color of the outer edges.

hdc) in corner ch-3 sp, *hdc in next 5 hdc, (hdc, ch 3, hdc) in next corner ch-3 sp; repeat from * 2 more times, hdc in next hdc; join with sl st in top of beginning ch. Fasten off first color—28 hdc and 4 ch-3 sp.

Outer Edges
Note: Work now proceeds, back and forth, in rows across only two sides of the inner square.
Row 4 With RS facing, join 2nd color with sl st in any corner ch-3 sp, ch 2, *hdc in next 7 hdc, (hdc, ch 3, hdc) in corner ch-3 sp, hdc in next 7 hdc, hdc in next corner ch-3 sp, turn—18 hdc and 1 ch-3 sp.
Rows 5–10 Ch 2, hdc in each hdc to corner ch-3 sp, (hdc, ch 3, hdc) in corner ch-3 sp, hdc in each hdc across, hdc in top of turning ch, turn—30 hdc and 1 ch-3 sp (at the end of Row 10). Fasten off.

Finishing
Arrange squares as shown in assembly diagram. Whipstitch squares together.

Edging
Rnd 1 With RS facing, join F with sc in any corner ch-3 sp, work 2 more sc in same ch-3 sp; sc evenly spaced across each side of blanket, working 3 sc in each corner ch-3 sp; join with sl st in first sc. Fasten off.
Rnd 2 With RS facing, join A with sl st in the first sc of any corner 3-sc group, ch 2, hdc in same sc, 2 hdc in next 2 sc of corner, hdc in each sc to next corner 3-sc group, *2 hdc in each sc of corner 3-sc group, hdc in each sc to next corner 3-sc group; repeat from * 2 more times; join with sl st in top of beginning ch. Fasten off. Using yarn needle, weave in all ends.
Block gently, if desired. ∎

Tunisian & Cable Blanket

An out-of-the-ordinary stitch pattern makes for an extraordinary addition to a wee one's layette.

Designed by Ellen Gormley

▬▬▬▬▬

Finished Measurements

Blanket measures approximately 32" x 36"/81.5cm x 91.5cm

Gauge

In cable strip pattern, 9 sts = 2"/5cm and 12 rows = 4"/10cm;
In Tunisian pattern, 13 sts and 12 rows = 4"/10cm.

Stitches Used

Chain (**ch**)
Single crochet (**sc**)
Slip stitch (**sl st**)

Special Stitches

FPdc: Front-post double crochet—Yarn over, insert hook from front to back and then to front again around post of indicated stitch 2 rows below, yarn over and draw up loop, [yarn over and draw through 2 loops on hook] twice. Skip the stitch behind the FPdc.

FPtr: Front-post treble crochet—[Yarn over] twice, insert hook from front to back and then to front again around post of indicated stitch 2 rows below, yarn over and draw up a loop, [yarn over and draw through 2 loops on hook] 3 times. Skip the stitch behind the FPtr.

Tks: Tunisian Knit Stitch—Insert hook under next vertical bar and from front to back through fabric, yarn over and draw up a loop.

Notes

1. Tunisian panels are worked with the RS facing at all times. Do not turn at ends of rows.
2. Each row of Tunisian crochet is worked in two steps: a forward pass and a return pass. The forward pass is worked from right to left with RS facing. Loops are picked up and

placed on the hook during the forward pass. The return pass is worked from left to right with RS facing. Loops are worked off the hook during the return pass.
3. Cable strips are worked with traditional hook, back and forth in rows.
4. All post stitches (FPdc and FPtr) are worked in stitches 2 rows below (one row below the stitches into which you would usually work). Always skip the stitch behind the post stitch.

Tunisian Panel (make 2)

With Afghan/Tunisian hook and A, ch 33.
Row 1 (RS)
Forward Pass With A, working from right to left, insert hook in 2nd ch from hook and draw up a loop, *insert hook in next ch and draw up a loop; repeat from * across. Do not turn—33 loops on hook.
Return Pass: With B, working from left to right, yarn over and draw through first loop

on hook, *yarn over and draw through 2 loops on hook; repeat from * across. Do not turn—1 loop remains on hook.
Row 2
Forward Pass With B, working from right to left, sk first vertical bar (at edge), *yarn over, sk next vertical bar, Tks; repeat from * across. Do not turn—33 loops on hook.
Return Pass: With C, working from left to right, yarn over and draw through first loop on hook, *yarn over and draw through 2 loops on hook; repeat from * across. Do not turn—1 loop remains on hook.
Row 3 Repeat Row 2; work forward pass with C, and return pass with A.
Row 4 Repeat Row 2; work forward pass with A, and return pass with B.
Rows 5–91 Repeat Rows 2–4 twenty-nine times.
Rows 92 and 93 Repeat Rows 2 and 3.
Row 94 (Tunisian bind off) Place remaining loop onto traditional crochet hook, sc in each space (formed by yarn overs of previous row) and through each vertical bar (as if for Tks) across—33 sc. Do not fasten off.

Edging (RS) Ch 1, work 94 sc evenly spaced across long edge, ch 1; working across opposite side of foundation ch, sc in each ch across, ch 1; work 94 sc evenly spaced across 2nd long edge, ch 1; join with sl st in first st of Row 94. Fasten off.

Cable Strip (make 3)

With traditional crochet hook and A, ch 10.
Row 1 (WS): Sc in 2nd ch from hook and in each remaining ch across, turn—9 sts.
Row 2 (RS): Ch 2 (counts as first dc here and

Choose a gender-neutral palette for a blanket fit for little kings and queens.

throughout), dc in each sc across, turn.

Row 3 Ch 1, sc in each dc across, turn.

Row 4 Ch 2, [FPdc around next dc 2 rows below, dc in next sc] 4 times, turn.

Row 5 Ch 1, sc in each st across, turn.

Note: Remember to skip the stitch behind a post stitch. Whenever a post stitch is worked, skip the next stitch in the row into which you would usually work stitches.

Row 6 Ch 2, FPdc around next FPdc 2 rows below, dc in next sc, sk next FPdc 2 rows below, FPtr around next FPdc 2 rows below, dc in next sc, FPtr around skipped FPdc 2 rows below (Cross made), dc in next sc, FPdc around next FPdc 2 rows below, dc in last sc, turn.

Row 7 Ch 1, sc in each st across, turn.

Row 8 Ch 2, [FPdc around next FPdc or FPtr 2 rows below, dc in next sc] 4 times, turn.

Rows 9–96 Repeat Rows 5–8 twenty-two times.

Row 97 Repeat Row 5. Fasten off.

Finishing

Assembly

With RS facing, arrange strips and panels, with long edges together, as follows: Cable Strip, Tunisian Panel, Cable Strip, Tunisian Panel, Cable Strip. Use locking stitch markers to hold strips in place. With RS facing, traditional crochet hook, and working through both thicknesses, join A with sl st at beginning of a long edge, ch 1, sc evenly spaced across long edge, to join a strip to a panel. Fasten off. Repeat this process to join all strips and panels together.

Edging

With RS facing and traditional crochet hook,

join A with sl st in corner of blanket, to work across top (a short edge).

Rnd 1 (RS) Ch 2 (counts as dc here and throughout), work 4 more dc in same corner, work 97 dc evenly spaced across top of blanket, 5 dc in corner, work 109 dc evenly spaced across side of blanket, 5 dc in corner, work 97 dc evenly spaced across lower edge of blanket, 5 dc in corner, work 109 dc evenly spaced across 2nd side of blanket; join with sl st in top of beginning ch-2—432 dc.

Note: In following rounds, the FPtr and FPdc are worked around stitches in row into which stitches are usually worked (one row below), not around stitches 2 rows below.

Rnd 2 Ch 2, dc in next dc, 5 dc in next dc (corner), [dc in next 3 dc, *sk next 2 dc, FPtr around next st, dc in last st skipped, FPtr around first st skipped (Cross made), dc in next st; repeat from * across to next corner 5-dc, dc in first 2 dc of corner 5-dc, 5 dc in next dc] 3 times, dc in next 3 dc, **sk next 2 dc, FPtr around next st, dc in last st skipped, FPtr around first st skipped, dc in next st; repeat from ** across to first corner; join with sl st in top of beginning ch-2. Do not turn.

Rnd 3 Ch 2, dc in next 3 dc, 5 dc in next dc (corner), [dc in next 5 dc, *FPdc around next FPtr, dc in next dc; repeat from * across to 2 dc before next corner 5-dc, dc in next 4 dc, 5 dc in next dc (corner)] 3 times, dc in next 5 dc, **FPdc around next FPtr, dc in next dc; repeat from ** across; join with sl st in top of beginning ch-2.

Rnd 4 Sl st in each st around. Fasten off.

Using yarn needle, weave in all ends. Block lightly, if desired. ∎

Granny's Cabin Blanket

Based on the traditional log cabin quilt pattern, this brightly colored country classic looks equally at home in a big-city nursery.

Designed by Renée Barnes

Finished Measurements

Blanket measures approximately 39" x 39"/99cm x 99cm

Gauge

In half double crochet, 14 sts and 10 rows = 4"/10cm.
Section 1 measures approximately 4" x 4"/10cm x 10cm.
Gauge is not critical for this project.

Stitches Used

Chain (**ch**)
Double crochet (**dc**)
Half double crochet (**hdc**)
Single crochet (**sc**)
Slip stitch (**sl st**)

What you'll need:

YARN
Caron International's Simply Soft Collection
(100% acrylic)
6 oz (A), 6 oz (B), 6 oz (C), 12 oz (D), 6 oz (E)
Shown in: #0017 Lemon (A), #0016 Melon (B),
#0015 Strawberry (C), #0004 Blueberry (D),
#0005 Blackberry (E)
CROCHET HOOK
One size US H-8 (5mm), or size to obtain gauge
ADDITIONAL MATERIALS
Yarn needle

Notes:
1. Each block begins with a square (section 1). A rectangle (section 2) is then worked across one side edge of the center square. The combined piece is given a ¼ turn clockwise, and another rectangle is worked across the side edge of the combined section 1 and section 2 piece. This process is continued until 9 sections have been worked. Refer to diagram for arrangement of the sections.
2. When working across the ends of rows, evenly space 7 hdc over 5 rows to match pattern.
3. Join all new colors with RS facing.

Block (make 9)

Section 1
With A, ch 15.
Row 1 (RS): Hdc in 3rd ch from hook (beginning ch counts as first hdc) and in each remaining ch across, turn—14 hdc.
Hint: Place marker on RS, for future reference.
Rows 2–10: Ch 2 (counts as first hdc here and throughout), hdc in each hdc across, turn. Fasten off.

Section 2
With RS facing, join B with sl st in any corner, to work in ends of rows across side edge of section 1.
Row 1: Ch 2, working in ends of rows, work 13 hdc evenly spaced across side edge, turn—14 hdc.
Rows 2–5: Ch 2, hdc in each hdc across, turn. Fasten off.

Section 3
With RS facing, give the piece a ¼ turn, and join C with sl st in corner, to work across side edge of section 2, and across top (or bottom) edge of section 1.
Row 1: Ch 2, work 20 hdc evenly spaced across edge, turn—21 hdc.
Rows 2–5: Ch 2, hdc in each hdc across, turn. Fasten off.

Section 4
With RS facing, give the piece a ¼ turn, and join D with sl st in corner, to work across side edge of section 3, and side edge of section 1.
Row 1: Ch 2, work 20 hdc evenly spaced across edge, turn—21 hdc.
Rows 2–5: Ch 2, hdc in each hdc across, turn. Fasten off.

Section 5
With RS facing, give the piece a ¼ turn, and join E with sl st in corner, to work across side edge of section 4, bottom (or top) edge of section 1, and side edge of section 2.
Row 1: Ch 2, work 27 hdc evenly spaced across edge, turn—28 hdc.
Rows 2–5: Ch 2, hdc in each hdc across, turn. Fasten off.

Section 6
With RS facing, give the piece a ¼ turn, and join C with sl st in corner, to work across side edge of section 5, top edge of section 2, and side edge of section 3.
Row 1: Ch 2, work 27 hdc evenly spaced across edge, turn—28 hdc.
Rows 2–5: Ch 2, hdc in each hdc across, turn. Fasten off.

Section 7
With RS facing, give the piece a ¼ turn, and join B with sl st in corner, to work across side edge of section 6, top edge of section 3, and side edge of section 4.
Row 1: Ch 2, work 34 hdc evenly spaced across edge, turn—35 hdc.
Rows 2–5: Ch 2, hdc in each hdc across, turn. Fasten off.

Section 8
With RS facing, give the piece a ¼ turn, and

join E with sl st in corner, to work across side edge of section 7, top edge of section 4, and side edge of section 5.

Row 1: Ch 2, work 34 hdc evenly spaced across edge, turn—35 hdc.

Rows 2–5: Ch 2, hdc in each hdc across, turn. Fasten off.

Section 9

With RS facing, give the piece a ¼ turn, and join D with sl st in corner, to work across side edge of section 8, top edge of section 5, and side edge of section 6.

Row 1: Ch 2, work 41 hdc evenly spaced across edge, turn—42 hdc.

Rows 2–5: Ch 2, hdc in each hdc across, turn.

Fasten off.

Edging

With RS facing, join D with sc in first hdc of section 9, 2 sc in same hdc (corner made), sc in each hdc across to last hdc, 3 sc in last hdc (corner made); [work 40 sc evenly spaced across next edge of block, 3 sc in next corner] twice, work 40 sc evenly spaced across last edge of block; join with sl st in first sc. Fasten off.

Finishing

With RS facing and all blocks with section 9 at top, arrange blocks into 3 rows of 3 blocks each. With yarn needle and D, whipstitch blocks together.

Border

Rnd 1: With RS facing, join A with sl st in any corner, ch 5 (counts as dc, ch 2), dc in same corner, dc in each st across side to corner, *(dc, ch 2, dc) in corner, dc in each st across side to next corner; repeat from * 2 more times; join with sl st in 3rd ch of beginning ch.

Rnds 2 and 3: Sl st into first ch-2 sp, ch 5, dc in same ch-2 sp, dc in each st across side to corner ch-2 sp, *(dc, ch 2, dc) in corner ch-2 sp, dc in each st across side to next corner; repeat from * 2 more times; join with sl st in 3rd ch of beginning ch. Fasten off.

Using yarn needle, weave in ends.

Block gently, if desired. ▪

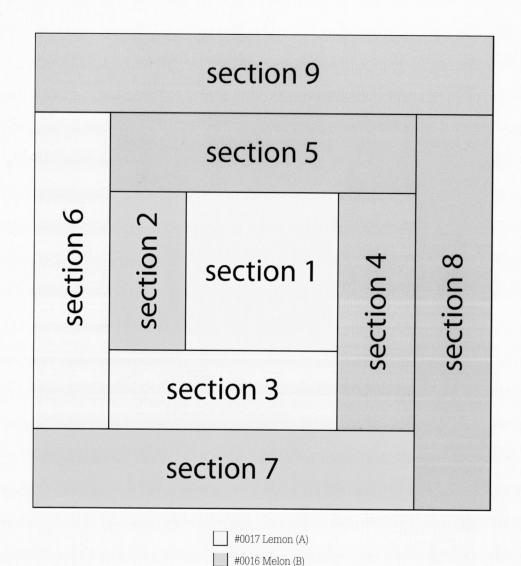

☐ #0017 Lemon (A)

☐ #0016 Melon (B)

☐ #0015 Strawberry (C)

☐ #0004 Blueberry (D)

☐ #0005 Blackberry (E)

Star Struck Blanket

Soothing shades of pink and peach and an eye-pleasing textured stitch make this throw the "star" of a favorite little girl's nursery.

Designed by Kimberley Biddix

Finished Measurements

Blanket measures approximately 32" x 40"/81.5 x 101.5cm, not including fringe

Gauge

In pattern, 4 StarSts and 5½ rows = 4"/10cm. *Gauge is not critical for this project.*

Stitches Used

Chain (**ch**)
Double crochet (**dc**)
Half double crochet (**hdc**)
Single crochet (**sc**)
Slip stitch (**sl st**)

Special Stitches

Beg-StarSt: Beginning Star Stitch— Ch 3, insert hook in 2nd ch from hook and draw up a loop (2 loops on hook), insert hook in next ch and draw up a loop (3 loops on hook), insert hook in first sc and draw up a loop (4 loops on hook), [insert hook in next sc and draw up a loop] twice, yarn over and draw through all 6 loops on hook, ch 1 to close star and form eyelet.

StarSt: Star Stitch—Insert hook in eyelet of last StarSt made and draw up a loop (2 loops

on hook), insert hook through last 2 loops on side of last StarSt made and draw up a loop (3 loops on hook), insert hook in same sc as last leg of last StarSt made and draw up a loop (4 loops on hook), [insert hook in next sc and draw up a loop] twice, yarn over and draw through all 6 loops on hook, ch 1, to close star and form eyelet.

Blanket

With one strand each of A, B, and C held together, ch 58.

Row 1: Sc in 2nd ch from hook and in each ch across, turn—57 sc.

Row 2 (RS): Beg-StarSt, *ch 1, StarSt; repeat from * across, turn—28 StarSts.

What you'll need:

YARN
Caron International's Simply Soft (100% acrylic)
18 oz (A), 18 oz (B), 18 oz (C)
Shown in: #9701 White (A), #9717 Orchid (B),
#9737 Light Country Peach (C)

CROCHET HOOK
One size US N-10 (15mm) hook, or size to obtain gauge

ADDITIONAL MATERIALS
Yarn needle

Row 3: Ch 1, 2 sc in eyelet of first StarSt, sc in the StarSt, *sc in eyelet of next StarSt, sc in the StarSt; repeat from * across, turn—57 sc.

Rows 4–49: Repeat last 2 rows 23 more times. Fasten off.

Finishing

Edging

Rnd 1: With RS facing and holding 3 strands of C together, join yarn with sl st in edge of blanket, sc evenly spaced around edge, working 3 sc in each corner; join with sl st in first sc. Fasten off.

Rnd 2: With B, repeat Round 1. Fasten off.

Rnd 3: With A, repeat Round 1. Fasten off. Using yarn needle weave in all ends.

Fringe

Cut strands of A, B, and C, 17"/43cm long. Holding 5 strands of one color together, fold fringe in half, and attach in every other st around edge of blanket, as follows:* Using crochet hook, insert hook from WS to RS into st, pull fold through forming a loop, insert ends into loop and pull tight against edge; repeat from * round edge of blanket, alternating the colors. Trim ends of fringe. ▪

Baby Loves Brights

Squares and rectangles of varying sizes and a
mixed palette of unexpected shades make this blanket
perfect for both boys and girls.

Designed by Randy Cavaliere

What you'll need:

YARN
Caron International's Simply Soft Collection (100% acrylic)
6 oz (A), 6 oz (B), 6 oz (c), 6 oz (D), 6 oz (E), 6 oz (F)
Shown in:
#0001 Vanilla (A), #0008 Autumn Maize (B),
#0007 Aqua Mist (C), #0004 Blueberry (D),
#0005 Blackberry (E), #0012 Passion (F)
CROCHET HOOKS
One size US M-13 (9mm), or size to obtain gauge
One size US L-11 (8mm) (for border only)
ADDITIONAL MATERIALS
Yarn needle

Finished Measurements
Blanket measures approximately
36" wide x 48" long (91.5cm x 122cm)

Gauge
Rounds 1–3 of center
square = 4"/10cm.
In single crochet, 8 sts and
10 rows = 4"/10cm.

Stitches Used
Chain (**ch**)
Double crochet (**dc**)
Half double crochet (**hdc**)
Single crochet (**sc**)
Slip stitch (**sl st**)

Special Term
Cl Cluster—Yarn over, insert hook in indicated st and draw up a loop, yarn over and
draw through 2 loops on hook; [yarn over,
insert hook in same st and draw up a loop,
yarn over and draw through 2 loops on
hook] twice; yarn over and draw through
all 4 loops on hook.
Note: All squares are worked with 2 strands
of yarn held together. When only one color is
listed, hold 2 strands of the same color together.

12"/30.5cm Center Square
(make 1)
With larger hook and 1 strand each of D
and E held together, ch 4; join with sl st in
first ch to form a ring.
Round 1 (RS) Ch 1, work 8 sc in ring; join
with sl st in first sc, turn—8 sc.
Rnd 2 Ch 3 (counts as first dc), 2 dc in same
st as join, ch 3, sk next sc, *3 dc in next sc, ch
3, sk next sc; repeat from * around; join with
sl st in top of turning ch, turn—12 dc and 4
ch-3 sp.
Rnd 3 Ch 3 (counts as first hdc, ch 1), (hdc,

ch 3, hdc) in next ch-3 sp (corner made), ch 1,
hdc in next dc, ch 1, sk next dc, *hdc in next
dc, ch 1, (hdc, ch 3, hdc) in next ch-3 sp (corner
made), ch 1, hdc in next dc, ch 1, sk next dc;
repeat from * around; join with sl st in 2nd ch
of turning ch, turn—16 hdc and 4 ch-3 sp.
Rnd 4 Ch 3 (counts as first hdc, ch 1), *[hdc in
next hdc, ch 1] across to next ch-3 sp, (2 hdc,
ch 2, 2 hdc) in next ch-3 sp, ch 1; repeat from
* 3 more times, [hdc in next hdc, ch 1] across
to end of round; join with sl st in 2nd ch of
turning ch, turn—32 hdc and 4 ch-2 sp.
Rnd 5 Ch 1, sc in same st as join, ch 1, sc in
next hdc, ch 1, sc in next 2 hdc, 3 sc in next
ch-2 sp, sc in next 2 hdc, *[ch 1, sc in next
hdc] across to next corner, ch 1, sc in next 2
hdc, 3 sc in next ch-2 sp, sc in next 2 hdc;
repeat from * 2 more times, ch 1, [sc in next
hdc, ch 1] to end of round; join with sl st in
first sc, turn—44 sc.
Rnd 6 Ch 4 (counts as first dc, ch 1), [dc in
next sc, ch 1] 3 times, sk next sc, dc in next sc,
ch 1, sk next sc, (dc, ch 3, dc) in next dc (corner), ch 1, sk next sc, dc in next sc, ch 1, *[dc
in next sc, ch 1] 5 times, sk next sc, dc in next

sc, ch 1, sk next sc, (dc, ch 3, dc)
in next dc, ch 1, sk next sc, dc in
next sc, ch 1; repeat from * 2
more times, dc in last sc, ch 1;
join with sl st in first dc, turn—36
dc, 32 ch-1 sp, and 4 ch-3 sp.
Rnd 7 Ch 1, *[sc in next ch-1 sp,
ch 1] across to next ch-3 sp, ([sc,
ch 1] twice, sc) in next ch-3 sp,
ch 1; repeat from * 3 more times,
[sc in next ch-1 sp, ch 1] 5 times;
join with sl st in first sc—44 sc,
and 44 ch-1 sp. Fasten off.
Rnd 8 (RS) With RS facing, join
yarn with sl st in center sc of any
corner, ch 3 (counts as first dc),
(dc, ch 3, 2 dc) in same sc, ch 2, sk
next sc, [Cl in next sc, ch 1, Cl in
next sc, ch 2, sk next sc] 3 times, *(2 dc, ch 3, 2
dc) in next sc, ch 2, sk next sc, [Cl in next sc, ch
1, Cl in next sc, ch 2, sk next sc] 3 times; repeat
from * around; join with sl st in top of turning
ch, turn—24 clusters, 16 dc, 16 ch-2 sp, 12 ch-1
sp and 4 ch-3 sp.
Rnd 9 Ch 3 (counts as first dc), dc in next
ch-2 sp, *ch 1, [dc in next Cl, ch 1] twice, dc
in next ch-2 sp; repeat from * across to next
corner, dc in next 2 dc, ch 1, (2 dc, ch 1, 2 dc)
in corner ch-3 sp, ch 1, **dc in next 2 dc, dc in
next ch-2 sp, {ch 1, [dc in next Cl, ch 1] twice,
dc in next ch-2 sp} across to next corner, dc
in next 2 dc, ch 1, (2 dc, ch 1, 2 dc) in corner
ch-3 sp, ch 1; repeat from ** to last dc, dc in
last dc; join with sl st in 3rd ch of turning ch,
turn—72 dc and 48 ch-1 sp.
Rnd 10 Ch 1, sc in same dc as join, ch 1, sk
next dc, sc in next ch-1 sp, ch 1, sk next dc, sc
in next dc, ch 1, (sc, ch 1, sc) in next ch-1 sp,
ch 1, sc in next dc, ch 1, sk next dc, sc in next
ch-1 sp, ch 1, sk next dc, sc in next dc, ch 1,
sk next dc, [sc in next ch-1 sp, ch 1, sk next
dc] 9 times, *sk next dc, sc in next dc, ch 1,

You can change the colors of the blocks to coordinate with your baby's nursery.

sk next dc, sc in next ch-1 sp, ch 1, sk next dc, sc in next dc, ch 1, (sc, ch 1, sc) in next ch-1 sp, ch 1, sc in next dc, ch 1, sk next dc, sc in next ch-1 sp, ch 1, sk next dc, sc in next dc, ch 1, sk next dc, [sc in next ch-1 sp, ch 1, sk next dc] 9 times; repeat from * around; join with sl st in first sc—68 sc and 68 ch-1 sp. Fasten off.

10"/25.5cm square (make 4)
With larger hook and 1 strand each of B and C held together, ch 4; join with sl st in first ch to form a ring.
Rnds 1–8 Work Rounds 1–8 of center square. Fasten off.

8"/20.5cm Square
(make 8—4 with 1 strand each of A and B held together, and 4 with 2 strands of A)
With larger hook and 2 strands held together, ch 4; join with sl st in first ch to form a ring.
Rnds 1–7 Work Rounds 1–7 of center square.
Fasten off.

6"/15cm Square (make 4)
With larger hook and 1 strand each of C and D held together, ch 4; join with sl st in first ch to form a ring.
Rnds 1–5 Work Rounds 1–5 of center square.
Fasten off.

4"/10cm Square
(make 26 – 8 each with 2 strands of D, E, and F, and 2 with 2 strands of B)
With larger hook and 2 strands of yarn held together, ch 4; join with sl st in first ch to form a ring.
Rnds 1–3 Work Rounds 1–3 of center square.
Fasten off.

2"/5cm Square
(make 28—8 each with 2 strands of B and E, and 4 each with 2 strands of A, C, and D)
With larger hook and 2 strands of yarn held together, ch 5.
Row 1 (RS) Sc in 2nd ch from hook and in each ch across, turn—4 sc.
Rows 2–5 Ch 1, sc in each sc across, turn.
Fasten off.

Finishing
Arrange squares as shown in assembly diagram, placing 2", 4", 6", and 8" squares with RS facing, and 10" and center 12" square with WS facing. Using 2 strands of coordinating yarn, sew squares together.

Border
With RS facing, smaller hook, and holding 2 strands of C together, join yarn with sl st in edge of blanket, ch 1, sc evenly all the way around the outer edge, working 5 sc in each corner; join with sl st in first sc.
Using yarn needle, weave in all ends. ∎

Assembly diagram

Row 1: 10" Square B/C | 4" Square F, 4" Square D | 8" Square A/B | 4" Square F, 4" Square D | 10" Square B/C

2" row: 2" Square C, 2" Square B | 2" Square D, 2" Square E | 2" Square D, 2" Square E | 2" Square B, 2" Square C

Row 2: 4" Square D, 4" Square E | 8" Square A | 4" Square B, 4" Square F | 8" Square A | 4" Square E, 4" Square D

Side squares: 2" Square B, 2" Square A, 2" Square E | 6" Square C/D | (center) | 6" Square C/D | 2" Square B, 2" Square A, 2" Square E

Row 3: 8" Square A/B | 4" Square E, 4" Square F, 4" Square E | Center 12" Square D/E | 4" Square E, 4" Square F, 4" Square E | 8" Square A/B

Side squares: 2" Square E, 2" Square A, 2" Square B | 6" Square C/D | 6" Square C/D | 2" Square E, 2" Square A, 2" Square B

Row 4: 4" Square D, 4" Square E | 8" Square A | 4" Square F, 4" Square B | 8" Square A | 4" Square E, 4" Square D

2" row: 2" Square C, 2" Square B | 2" Square E, 2" Square D, 2" Square E | 2" Square D, 2" Square B, 2" Square C

Row 5: 10" Square B/C | 4" Square D, 4" Square F | 8" Square A/B | 4" Square D, 4" Square F | 10" Square B/C

Samara Blanket

A pretty repeating fan pattern is edged with a striking border in this traditional take on the baby blanket. Worked in a soothing creamy shade, it's perfect for newborns.

Designed by Darlene Dale

Finished Measurements

Blanket measures approximately 32" wide x 39" long (81.5cm x 99cm)

Gauge

1 shell (7 dc in same space) = 2"/5cm.

Stitches Used

Chain (**ch**)
Double crochet (**dc**)
Single crochet (**sc**)
Slip stitch (**sl st**)

Special Terms

puff st [Yarn over, insert hook in next st, yarn over, draw yarn through st, yarn over, draw yarn through 2 loops on hook] twice in same st, yo, draw yarn through 3 loops on hoop.
shell 7 dc in same space.
large shell (3 dc, ch 3, 3 dc) in same space.

Blanket

Ch 95.
Row 1 (WS) Sc in 5th ch from hook, *ch 3, skip next 3 ch, sc in next ch; rep from * across to within last 2 ch, ch 1, skip next ch, dc in last ch, turn—22 ch-3 spaces.
Row 2 Ch 1, sc in first dc, skip next ch-1 space, *shell in next ch-3 loop**, sc in next ch-3 loop, ch 3, sc in next ch-3 loop; rep from * across, ending last rep at **, skip next ch of turning ch, sc in next ch of turning ch, turn—8 shells.
Row 3 Ch 5 (counts as dc, ch 2), skip first 2

dc of shell, *sc in next dc, ch 3, skip next dc, sc in next dc**, ch 3, (puff st, ch3, puff st) in next ch-3 space, ch 3, skip next 3 sts; rep from * across, ending last rep at **, ch 2, skip next 2 dc, dc in last sc, turn—29 ch-3 spaces.
Row 4 Ch 1, sc in first dc, skip next ch-2 space, *shell in next ch-3 space**, skip next ch-3 loop, sc in next puff st, ch 3, skip next ch-3 space, sc in next puff st, skip next ch-3 space; rep from* across, ending last rep at **, skip next 2 ch of turning ch, sc in next ch of turning ch, turn.
Rep rows 3-4 until blanket measures 28"/71cm from beginning, ending with row 3 of patt. Do not fasten off.

Border

Rnd 1 (RS) Ch 1, working across top edge, work 93 sc evenly space across to next corner, sc in next corner, working across side edge, work 109 sc evenly spaced across to

What you'll need:

YARN
Naturally Caron Country
(75% acrylic, 25% merino wool)
Shown in: #0007 Naturally (14 oz)

CROCHET HOOK
One size US I-9 (5.5mm), or size to obtain gauge

ADDITIONAL MATERIALS
4 stitch markers
Yarn needle

next corner, sc in next corner; rep from * once, ending with last sc in same dc as first sc, join with sl st in first sc—396 sc.
Row 2 Ch 1, sc in each sc around, working 3 sc in the center sc in each corner, join with sl st in first sc—404 sc.
Rnd 3 Ch 1, sc in first sc, *ch 6, skip next 3 sc, sc in next sc; rep from * around, join with sl st to first sc—23 spaces across top and bottom edges; 27 spaces across each side edge; 1 space at each corner. Place marker in each corner space and move marker up as work progresses.
Rnd 4 Sl st to center of first ch-6 space, ch 1, sc in same ch-6 space, ch 2, *large shell in next ch-6 space, ch 2, sc in next ch-6 space, ch 2; rep from * around, join with sl st in first sc—11 large shells across top and bottom edges; 13 large shells across each side edge; 1 large shell at each corner.
Rnd 5 Ch 1, sc in first sc, ch 2, *skip next ch-2 space, large shell in next ch-3 space, ch 2, skip next ch-2 space, sc in next sc, ch 2; rep from * around, join with sl st in first sc.
Rnds 6-8 Ch 1, sc in first sc, *ch 2, skip next ch-2 space, large shell in next ch-3 space, ch 2, skip next ch-2 space, sc in next sc; rep from * across to sc before corner shell, ch 4, (4 dc, ch 4, 4 dc) in next corner ch-3 space, ch 4**, sc in next sc; rep from * around, ending last rep at **, join with sl st in first sc. Fasten off. Weave in ends and block to measurements. ∎

Posies Blanket

Lovely shades of lilac and blue worked in rows of floral motifs make the most beguiling baby blanket for a pretty little girl.

Designed by Andrea Graciarena

Finished Measurements

Blanket measures approximately 35½" long x 35½" wide (90cm x 90cm)

Gauge

3 posies and 9 rows = 7"/18cm

Stitches Used

Chain (**ch**), double crochet (**dc**), single crochet (**sc**), slip stitch (**sl st**)

Special Terms

cluster [Yarn over, insert hook in next st, yarn over and draw up a loop, yarn over and draw through 2 loops on hook] twice in same st or space, yarn over and draw through all 3 loops on hook.

Fl center space Flower center-space—turn, skip next 4 clusters, dc in next ch-3 space, turn.

H-Fl center space Half Flower center-space—turn, skip next 2 clusters, hdc in next ch-3 space, turn.

shell ([cluster, ch 2] 3 times, cluster) in same space.

half shell (cluster, ch 2, cluster) in same space.

Note:

The edging is worked with color A. To change color at end of row: Work last stitch of old color to last yarn over, yarn over with new color and draw through all loops on hook to complete stitch. Drop old color, continue work with new color. You may fasten off the old color (recommended for color B) or carry it loosely up the side of the piece. If you choose to carry unused colors up the side of the piece, take care to cover these strands when working the border.

Blanket

With A, ch 141.

Row 1 Sc in 6th ch from hook (counts as first ch-2 space),*ch 2, skip next 2 ch, sc in next ch; rep from * across, turn—46 ch-2 spaces.

Row 2 Ch 4 (counts as dc, ch 1 here and throughout), half shell in first ch-2 space, ch 1, skip next ch-2 space, sc in next sc, *ch 1, skip next ch-2 space**, shell in next ch-2 space, ch 1, skip next ch-2 space, sc in next sc; rep from * across, ending last rep at **, half shell in last ch-2 space, ch 1, dc in last sc, complete last st with B, drop A, turn—14 shells plus 2 half shells.

Row 3 With B, ch 1, sc in first sc, *ch 3, cluster in next cluster, skip next ch-2 space, cluster in next cluster, skip next 2 ch-1 spaces, cluster in next cluster, skip next ch-2 space, cluster in next cluster, turn, skip next 4 clusters, dc in next ch-3, turn (Fl center space made), ch 3, sc in next ch-2 space; rep from * across, ending with last sc in 3rd ch of turning ch, turn.

Row 4 Ch 1, sc in first sc, *ch 1, skip next ch-3 space, shell in next Fl center space, ch 1, skip next ch-3 space, sc in next sc; rep from * across, complete last st with A, drop B, turn—15 shells.

Row 5 With A, ch 3, *cluster in next cluster, skip next ch-2 space, cluster in next cluster, turn, skip next 2 clusters, hdc in next ch-3 space, turn (H-Fl center space made), ch 3, sc in next ch-2 space, *ch 3, cluster in next cluster, skip next ch-2 space, cluster in next cluster**, skip 2 ch-1 spaces, cluster in next cluster, skip next ch-2 space, cluster in next cluster, turn, skip next 4 clusters, dc in next ch-3 space, turn (Fl center space made), ch 3, sc in next ch-2 space; rep from * across, ending last rep at **, turn, skip next 2 clusters, hdc in next ch-3 space, turn (H-Fl center space made), dc in last sc, turn.

Row 6 Ch 4, half shell in next H-Fl center space, ch 1, sc in next sc, *ch 1, skip next ch-3 space **, shell in next Fl center space, ch 1, skip next ch-3 space, sc in next sc; rep from * across, ending last rep at **, half shell in next H-Fl center space, ch 1, dc in top of turning ch, turn—14 shells plus 2 half shells.

Rows 7–49 Rep rows 3-6 ten times, then rep Rows 3–5 once more.

Row 50 Ch 3 (counts as sc, ch 2), skip next H-Fl center space, sc in next ch-3 space at base of hdc, *ch 2, skip next ch-3 space, sc in next sc, ch 2, skip next ch-3 space**, sc in top of dc (Fl center space), ch 2, sc in base of same dc; rep from * across, ending last rep at **, sc in top of next hdc (H-Fl center space), ch 2, sc in top of turning ch at base of same hdc, turn—46 ch-2 spaces. Do not fasten off.

Edging

Rnd 1 Sl st to next ch-2 corner space, [ch 2, dc, ch 2, cluster] in same ch-2 corner space, *ch 1, skip next ch-2 space, sc in next sc, ch 1, skip next ch-2 space**, shell in next ch-2 space; rep from * across to next corner, ending last rep at **, ([cluster, ch 2] 5 times, cluster) in next ch-2 corner space, ***ch 1, sc in next 2 sc, ch 1****, shell in next H-Fl Center space***; rep from *** to *** across to next corner, ending last rep at****, ([cluster, ch 2] 5 times, cluster) in next ch-2 corner space, *****ch 1, skip next ch-2 space, sc in ch at base of next sc, ch 1, skip next ch-2 space******, shell in next ch-2 space; rep from ***** across to next corner ending last rep at ******, ([cluster, ch 2] 5 times, cluster) in next ch-2 corner space; rep from *** to *** across to last corner, ending last rep at ****, shell in last ch-2 corner space, ch 2, join with slip st in top of beg dc. Fasten off both colors. Weave in ends, block to finished measurements. ∎

What you'll need:

YARN
Caron International's Simply Soft Collection (100% acrylic)
12 oz (A), 12 oz (B)
Shown in: #9717 Orchid (A), #9715 Soft Blue (B)

CROCHET HOOK
One size US I-9 (5.5mm), or size to obtain gauge

ADDITIONAL MATERIALS
Yarn needle